DARKWEB
Between Anonymity, Freedom and Criminality

The term "dark web" often arouses curiosity and fear. What is really hidden behind this mysterious part of the internet? And how is the "deep web" different from what we call the "surface web"? In this comprehensive guide, we'll explore these worlds, clarify the differences, identify useful tools for navigating them, and discuss the associated opportunities and risks. Knowing the dark and deep web is a double-edged sword: it allows you to understand the world of online anonymity and security, but also to recognize and avoid the dangers that are part of it.

The goal of this eBook is to offer a comprehensive overview of the deep web and the dark web, providing the information you need to understand how to access these resources safely, what opportunities are available, and what ethical and legal risks are associated. We will also turn to the concepts of online privacy and anonymity, to give a well-rounded understanding of the phenomenon.

Target Audience

This guide is designed for those who want to better understand the hidden parts of the Internet, whether out of personal curiosity, or for those who deal with cybersecurity, investigative journalism, or want to learn how to have a more conscious and secure approach to their online privacy.

Main Chapters

Chapter 1: Introduction to the Deep Web and the Dark Web

- Differences between surface web, deep web, and dark web
- Structure of the Internet: Levels and Accessibility
- Importance of the Deep Web in the Modern IT Landscape

Chapter 2: Accessing the Deep Web and Dark Web

- Login browsers: Tor, I2P, and Freenet
- Installation and configuration of the main access tools
- Basics of Safe Browsing

Chapter 3: Anonymity and Privacy Tools

- VPNs, Proxies, and Their Roles in Security
- Encryption and data protection tools
- Practical tips to avoid traceability

Chapter 4: Opportunities of the Dark Web

- Hidden Communities and Forums: Shared Knowledge and Cooperation
- Bright Side of the Dark Web: Anonymous Communication for Activists and Journalists
- Legal markets: Available resources and how to use them to your advantage

Chapter 5: Risks of the Dark Web

- Scam, malware, and other threats
- Illegal activities: Drugs, weapons, counterfeiting and illicit services
- Legal and moral consequences of using the dark web

Chapter 6: Cybersecurity and Identity Protection

- Defense against malware and other attacks
- How to recognize and avoid phishing and scams
- Control of personal information and data breach

Chapter 7: How to Recognize Opportunities on the Dark Web

- Journalistic information: Finding hidden sources
- Protection of privacy in repressive contexts
- Legitimate Opportunities for Cybersecurity Specialists

Chapter 8: Ethical and Legal Side

- The line between legal and illegal on the deep and dark web
- Ethics of the use of anonymity tools
- Personal and moral responsibility in the use of technology

Chapter 9: Practical Navigation and Case Studies

- Step-by-step guides to safe navigation
- Case studies of legitimate use of the dark web
- Common mistakes and how to avoid them

Practical examples

- How to set up Tor and browse safely
- Study of an anonymous forum of activists
- Access to hidden sites to search for documents and resources

Appendices

- Glossary of top terms (Tor, VPN, Onion Routing, etc.)
- Additional resources: Useful links and recommended reading
- Current legislation relating to online anonymity and privacy

Technical Insights

- Anonymous routing protocols and encryption
- Tor architecture and how node anonymization works

Introduction to the Deep Web and the Dark Web

Differences between Surface Web, Deep Web, and Dark Web

The **surface web** represents the visible part of the Internet, the one we all use on a daily basis. It is accessible through search engines such as Google or Bing and consists of pages and content that do not require authentication to be displayed. However, this layer represents only a small portion of the internet, estimated at around 4-5% of all available content. Most of the sites we visit every day, such as news, social media, and informational pages, are part of the surface web, and it's what we often associate with the internet in general. However, its accessibility and indexing makes it vulnerable to censorship and traceability.

The **deep web** includes all that information that is not indexed by search engines. This includes academic data, company archives, password-protected pages, databases, government documents, emails, medical records, and more. The deep web is not dangerous or illegal by its nature, but it is simply not public. Access requires specific knowledge or special credentials. Most of the deep web is made up of content that needs to remain confidential or that is designed for specific users, such as academic databases or internal business systems. This part of the web is essential to ensure privacy and protection of data that should not be exposed publicly.

The **dark web** is a small part of the deep web, and can only be accessed through specific software, such as the Tor, I2P, or Freenet browser. Dark web content is purposely hidden and often requires anonymity, including black markets, crypto forums, and other assets that don't want to be publicly visible. Not everything found on the dark web is illegal, but many of its uses are often associated with clandestine activities. However, the dark web can also be used for legitimate purposes, such as protecting activists or journalists in countries with heavy censorship, making it a useful tool for anyone who needs to communicate securely and anonymously.

Structure of the Internet: Levels and Accessibility

- **Level 1: Surface Web** - The portion of the internet that is freely accessible by standard browsers and indexed by search engines. It includes sites like Wikipedia, Facebook, and most blogs and public forums. It is the part of the internet that represents the visible face of what we use every day, but it is limited in its depth and ability to access specialized information.
- **Level 2: Deep Web** - Includes all content that is not indexed by search engines for security and privacy reasons. This layer often requires authentication, and includes content such as cloud storage services, private pages, academic databases, and business documents. The deep web plays a critical role in maintaining the confidentiality of sensitive documents and hosting content that is not intended for indiscriminate public viewing.
- **Level 3: Dark Web** - It is a subsection of the deep web, accessible only with particular tools such as Tor. It contains content that is deliberately hidden and often related to anonymity issues, including legal activities (such as anonymous communication for journalists and activists) and illegal activities. The dark web represents a corner of the internet where risk and opportunity coexist, offering a space for both the protection of freedom of expression and illicit activities.

Importance of the Deep Web in the Modern IT Landscape

- **Practical Utility**: The deep web is home to most of the data available on the internet, including academic data and business archives. This is essential to protect information that

must remain confidential or has limited public domain value. Academic archives, for example, contain valuable research that must only be available to a select audience, while sensitive company information cannot be publicly disclosed for security and competitive reasons.
- **Privacy and Security**: Many users prefer to use the deep web to avoid traceability. For example, journalists, political activists, and people operating in repressive contexts use tools found on the deep and dark web to avoid censorship and communicate freely. The ability to access these resources without being tracked is crucial for the safety of those seeking to avoid state surveillance or other forms of control that limit freedom of expression.
- **Research and Innovation**: Many resources available on the deep web are of great importance for scientific and technological research. Archives, scientific publications, and research papers are generally available in depth to avoid copyright issues or illegal distribution. These archives represent an important reservoir of knowledge that can be used by researchers and academics to deepen scientific and technological studies, without the risk of infringing copyrights or incurring other legal issues.

In addition, the deep web is crucial for the protection of personal data, as it allows you to maintain a certain confidentiality for information that is not intended for public sharing. Financial institutions also make extensive use of the deep web to ensure the security of transactions and private communications between their customers.

Access to the Deep Web and Dark Web

Introduction to Deep Web and Dark Web Access

Accessing the deep web and dark web is not an impossible feat, but it does require an understanding of the tools and techniques needed to ensure security and anonymity. Unlike the surface web, these parts of the internet can't be explored by simply typing a URL into a regular browser like Chrome or Firefox. Throughout this chapter, we will examine the main technologies for safely accessing these hidden sections of the web, highlighting the differences between the deep web and the dark web, and discussing the various tools for identity protection.

Login Browsers: Tor, I2P, and Freenet

- **Tor Browser**
    - **What is Tor?** Tor (The Onion Router) is the most well-known and commonly used browser to access the dark web. It is designed to allow anonymity while browsing, hiding the user's identity via a distributed network of nodes. Every time you visit a site through Tor, your connection is routed through a series of nodes that make it difficult to track your location or identity.
    - **Installation and Configuration**: To access Tor, you need to download the Tor Browser from the official website. After installation, the browser works similarly to a regular web browser, with the only difference being that the connections are encrypted and anonymous.
    - **Safe Browsing with Tor**: While Tor provides very strong protection, it's still important to take extra precautions. Avoid accessing sites with personal credentials or downloading files from the Dark Web, as these can compromise your security.
- **I2P (Invisible Internet Project)**
    - **What is I2P?** I2P is a network that allows users to communicate securely and anonymously. Unlike Tor, which is geared towards anonymous web browsing, I2P is designed to provide a private, decentralized network for communication between users. It's less well known than Tor, but it offers an advanced level of anonymity for messaging and file sharing.
    - **Installation and Setup**: To use I2P, you need to download and install the software from the official website of I2P. Once configured, hidden services within the I2P network, known as "eepsites," can be accessed.
    - **Typical Uses of I2P**: I2P is often used for secure messaging and peer-to-peer file sharing and is especially useful for those looking for a more secure alternative to communicate without being surveilled.
- **Freenet**
    - **What is Freenet?** Freenet is a decentralized network that allows users to share files, publish websites, and communicate anonymously. It was developed to resist censorship and ensure freedom of expression. Freenet is designed to provide a platform for the free exchange of information, without the risk of censorship by authorities.
    - **Installation and Setup**: Freenet can be downloaded from the official website and requires specific configuration to establish a secure connection. After installation, you can join the network and access content shared by other users.
    - **Security and Privacy on Freenet**: Freenet uses strong encryption to ensure user privacy and the security of shared data. It is particularly suitable for anonymous document sharing and for publishing content without the fear of censorship.

Basics of Safe Browsing

- **VPN and Proxy**: Before accessing the deep web or dark web, it is advisable to use a VPN (Virtual Private Network) to add an extra layer of anonymity. VPNs encrypt your traffic and hide your IP address, making it much harder to trace you back to you. A proxy can also be used to route your connection, but it doesn't offer the same level of security as a VPN.
- **Precautions When Browsing**: Never provide personal information, do not access websites that ask for sensitive data, and do not download files without verifying their authenticity. The dark web is fraught with risks, and taking preventative measures is essential to maintain your security.
- **Data Encryption**: Use encryption tools to protect your data while browsing the deep and dark web. Programs like VeraCrypt can be used to encrypt sensitive files, ensuring that your information remains protected even in the event of unauthorized access.

Legal and Ethical Considerations of Access

Accessing the deep web and dark web is not illegal in itself, but the way these tools are used can lead to serious legal consequences. Much of the content on the dark web is related to illegal activities, such as drug trafficking, weapons, and other illicit services. It is important to understand the local laws regarding access to and use of anonymity tools, and to remember that any illegal activity will be severely punished.

From an ethical point of view, the dark web offers both opportunities for good and evil. On the one hand, it is a tool of protection for those living under oppressive regimes and need a secure platform to communicate. On the other hand, it hosts criminal activities that exploit the lack of ability to act outside the law. As users, it's crucial to make informed choices and use these tools responsibly.

Anonymity and Privacy Tools

Introduction to Anonymity and Privacy Tools

To browse the deep web and dark web securely, it is essential to have tools that provide a high level of anonymity and privacy. These tools are designed to protect user data, hide identity, and minimize the risk of being tracked. In this chapter, we'll explore in detail some of the key solutions available to protect your online identity, including VPNs, proxies, anonymous browsers, and encryption software.

VPN (Virtual Private Network)

- **What is a VPN?** A VPN, or Virtual Private Network, is a service that allows users to establish a secure and encrypted connection over the internet. By using a VPN, the user's IP address is hidden and replaced with an IP address from the VPN server, thus ensuring anonymity.
- **Benefits of a VPN**
    - **Data Encryption**: All data that is transmitted and received is encrypted using advanced security protocols, such as AES (Advanced Encryption Standard), which ensures a high level of protection. This process makes it extremely difficult for third parties to intercept the information, even if they were to gain access to the data stream. Each packet of data is encrypted point-to-point, and encryption keys are regularly renewed to prevent any key compromise attacks. Encryption also includes protection against Man-in-the-Middle (MITM) attacks, ensuring that data is not altered or viewed during its transfer.
    - **Hide Your Identity**: A VPN masks your IP address, making it difficult to trace your real location. Internet traffic is routed through a remote server, making the user's IP address visible as belonging to the VPN server, rather than the original device. This process significantly reduces the chances of tracking, especially if the VPN server is located in a different country. Additionally, many VPNs include advanced features such as a kill switch, which automatically cuts off your internet connection if the VPN disconnects, preventing the real IP address from being leaked. It's important to select a VPN that doesn't keep activity logs to ensure that no trace of your traffic is recorded or retained.
    - **Access to restricted content**: VPNs can be used to access sites and content that are blocked in certain geographic areas. For example, streaming platforms like Netflix, Hulu, or BBC iPlayer have content that is only available in certain regions. By using a VPN, you can simulate being in a specific geographic area, thus unblocking restricted content. VPNs are often used to bypass internet censorship in countries where access to certain websites is restricted or blocked, ensuring freedom of information and the ability to use otherwise inaccessible services. However, some streaming services are becoming increasingly adept at detecting and blocking VPN use, often requiring constant updating of VPN features to ensure continued access.
- **Setting up a VPN**: Setting up a VPN is usually straightforward. Once you've chosen a VPN service provider (such as NordVPN, ExpressVPN, or ProtonVPN), simply download the app, install it, and select a server to use. It is recommended to choose servers in countries with strong privacy regulations for added protection.

Proxy

- **What is a Proxy?** A proxy acts as an intermediary between your computer and the website you want to visit. When using a proxy, requests are routed through a proxy server, which makes your IP address hidden from the target site. In other words, the proxy server makes the request to the website on your behalf, so the website will see the proxy's IP address instead of yours. Proxies can be configured for a variety of purposes, including bypassing geo-restrictions, filtering content, or improving connection speed through the cache. There are various types of proxies, such as HTTP proxies, which work at the web protocol level, and SOCKS proxies, which are more versatile and can be used for different applications beyond just web browsing. However, it's important to note that proxies don't encrypt traffic, which means that your activities could still be intercepted by third parties, especially if you're not using a secure connection (HTTPS).
- **Differences Between VPN and Proxy**: While both proxies and VPNs can hide the IP address, proxies do not encrypt the user's traffic like a VPN does. VPN uses strong encryption protocols to protect all communications, while proxies simply reroute traffic without adding a layer of cryptographic protection. This makes proxies suitable for light web browsing and accessing geographically blocked content, but less secure than a VPN for sensitive activities. Also, while a VPN protects all outgoing traffic from your device, a proxy generally only works with specific applications, such as your browser, and doesn't offer total protection for all network traffic.
- **When to Use a Proxy**: Proxies can be useful when you want to quickly access blocked content, such as geo-restricted websites, or to bypass filters imposed by local networks (such as school or corporate networks). Additionally, proxies are useful for tasks that do not require a high level of security, such as accessing media content that is restricted in certain regions. However, they are not the best solution for overall privacy and security, as they do not encrypt traffic and do not protect against possible eavesdropping by third parties. For activities involving sensitive data, such as financial transactions or private communications, it's best to use a VPN or more advanced encryption tools.

Anonymous Browser

- **Tor Browser**: As discussed in the previous chapter, the Tor Browser is the primary tool for accessing the dark web. It is designed to ensure anonymity by routing user traffic through a series of random nodes within the Tor network, which offer multiple layers of encryption. Each node only knows the address of the previous node and the address of the next node, making it virtually impossible to reconstruct the full path of the connection. Traffic is encrypted in multiple layers (hence the term 'Onion Routing'), and each node removes only one layer of encryption, ensuring incremental security at each step. Tor Browser also includes browser fingerprinting protection features, making it difficult for websites to identify the user's system.
    - **Security Tips**: To maximize security while using Tor, avoid performing insecure downloads and do not enter personal information while browsing. Use a VPN in conjunction with Tor to add an extra layer of protection. Please disable JavaScript, as it may be exploited to compromise your privacy. Make sure you only use sites with enough reputation and don't click on suspicious links. Finally, avoid making any financial transactions while browsing Tor, as it may expose your sensitive data.
- **Alternatives to Tor**: There are also other browsers and tools that promise a level of anonymity, such as Brave, which includes advanced privacy features and an integration with Tor for anonymous browsing.

Encryption Tools

- **Encrypting Files with VeraCrypt**
    - **What is VeraCrypt?** VeraCrypt is an open-source tool for encrypting files and folders. It can be used to create encrypted volumes to store sensitive data. VeraCrypt uses strong encryption algorithms, such as AES, Serpent, and Twofish, which ensure a high level of security. These algorithms are combined to offer multiple encryption options, making it extremely difficult for attackers to decrypt. The encryption offered by VeraCrypt is extremely robust and can protect your information even if your device is stolen. In addition, VeraCrypt allows the creation of hidden volumes within other encrypted volumes, a technique called 'plausible deniability', which allows sensitive data to be further protected in the event of coercion. This makes VeraCrypt a particularly suitable tool for protecting critical personal and business data.
    - **Common Uses of VeraCrypt**: Many users use VeraCrypt to protect backups of data, financial documents, and any other information that requires extreme protection. For example, businesses and freelancers can use it to protect sensitive client data or confidential information about ongoing projects. In addition, VeraCrypt is often used to protect physical storage media, such as external hard drives and USB sticks, especially during transport, reducing the risk of crucial information falling into the wrong hands if lost or stolen. Another common use is for the protection of legal documents or scientific research materials, where confidentiality is of utmost importance. The ability to create hidden volumes is particularly appreciated by activists and journalists who operate in high-risk contexts and need additional protection for data that could be sought in the event of an audit.
- **PGP (Pretty Good Privacy)**
    - **What is PGP?** PGP (Pretty Good Privacy) is a very strong encryption method used primarily to protect email communications, but it can also be applied to files and data. PGP uses a public and private key encryption system, in which the sender encrypts the message using the recipient's public key, and only the recipient with his private key can decrypt it. This mechanism provides a high level of security because, even if the encrypted message were intercepted, it could not be read without the correct private key. PGP, in addition to encryption, also provides digital signature functions, allowing the recipient to verify the authenticity of the sender and ensure that the message has not been altered during transport. This system is based on a web of trust infrastructure, in which users can certify each other's identity, adding an additional layer of security.
    - **Uses of PGP**: PGP is especially useful for those who communicate via email about sensitive topics and want to ensure that only the legitimate recipient can read the content of the message. To use PGP, the user must first generate a key pair: a public key and a private key. The public key can be shared freely with anyone who wants to send them an encrypted message, while the private key must be kept secret in order to decrypt the messages received. Once PGP software is installed, such as GnuPG or a PGP-enabled email client (such as Thunderbird with the Enigmail extension), the user can encrypt messages with the recipient's public key and digitally sign messages to ensure authenticity. The recipient then uses their private key to decrypt the message. The use of PGP requires careful management of keys and digital signatures, to prevent compromised keys from jeopardizing the security of communications. In addition, the user must verify the authenticity of public keys through secure methods, such as direct exchanges or the use of the 'web of trust'.

Additional Privacy Precautions

- **Password Management**: Use a reputable password manager (such as Bitwarden or LastPass) to generate and store strong passwords. Strong passwords are one of the first lines of defense against hacking attempts.
- **Disable JavaScript**: When browsing the dark web, it is advisable to disable JavaScript since it can be used to carry out attacks that compromise user anonymity and security. JavaScript, in fact, can be exploited to collect information about the system, such as the real IP address, the type of device and the characteristics of the browser, making it possible to fingerprint the user. Many dark web sites contain malicious scripts designed to bypass anonymity protections and execute malicious code directly in the browser. Disabling JavaScript significantly reduces the risk of exploits based on browser vulnerabilities or advanced tracking techniques. Tor Browser users can disable JavaScript directly through security settings, increasing the level of protection and choosing the "Maximum Security Level" mode to block scripts and other potentially dangerous content.
- **HTTPS connections**: Make sure to always use HTTPS to ensure a secure connection between your browser and the website. HyperText Transfer Protocol Secure (HTTPS) uses an encrypted connection that prevents third parties from intercepting or modifying data during transfer. There are browser extensions like HTTPS Everywhere, which force the use of HTTPS when available, ensuring that every connection is established securely. The use of HTTPS is especially important when transmitting sensitive data, such as login credentials, financial information, or other personal information. Be sure to check for the padlock in your browser's address bar, which indicates that your connection is secure. Additionally, you should avoid entering sensitive data on sites that do not use HTTPS, as these may be vulnerable to Man-in-the-Middle (MITM) attacks or other eavesdropping techniques.

Dark Web Opportunities

Introduction to Dark Web Opportunities

The dark web is often perceived only as a place for illicit activity, but it also offers several legitimate opportunities for those who know how to exploit them. In this chapter, we will explore the positives and opportunities present on the dark web, including discussion forums, resources for journalism, privacy tools, and even legal markets. To find these resources, it is essential to use access tools such as the Tor browser, which allows you to browse anonymously, and search engines specific to the dark web such as DuckDuckGo or Ahmia. In addition, many of the most reliable resources are shared in trusted forums; So, it's important to build a network of contacts and references to access direct links. The Dark Web, in fact, can be an important place for accessing free and uncensored information, making it a reference point for journalists, activists, and anyone who wants to protect their privacy online.

Hidden Communities and Forums: Shared Knowledge and Cooperation

- **Anonymous Discussion Forums**: The dark web is home to a wide range of anonymous discussion forums that cover every possible topic. These forums allow users to share information freely, without the fear of censorship or tracking. This is especially important for those living in countries where freedom of expression is restricted. In these spaces, users can discuss technology, privacy, scientific research, politics, and other sensitive topics without worrying about legal or social repercussions.
- **Collaboration between Activists and Researchers**: For activists operating in high-risk contexts, anonymous forums on the dark web offer a place for sharing security strategies and organizing joint actions. Researchers can also exchange information on vulnerabilities and protection methods, fostering a shared security culture and making it possible to develop new solutions to protect online privacy.

The Bright Side of the Dark Web: Anonymous Communication for Activists and Journalists

- **Safe Reporting Platforms**: The dark web is used as a secure platform for reporting abuse and corruption. Many newspapers and international organizations, such as WikiLeaks, have created secure communication channels on the dark web to allow whistleblowers to send confidential documents without compromising their identity. This form of communication is essential in countries where investigative journalism is subject to repression and censorship.
- **Freedom of Information Protection**: Journalists covering sensitive topics, such as government corruption, human trafficking, or human rights violations, can use the dark web to securely communicate with their sources. The dark web offers a level of anonymity that allows sources to share information without fear of detection, thus increasing the likelihood of important information reaching the public.

Legal Markets: Available Resources and How to Exploit Them

- **Buying Books and Digital Content**: Some marketplaces on the dark web allow you to buy legal digital content, such as books and publications that may be censored on the surface web. These marketplaces allow content to be purchased without leaving digital traces, thus ensuring greater privacy.
- **Software and Privacy Tools**: Legal dark web marketplaces also offer a variety of software, such as encryption tools and VPNs, that help users protect their identity. In some cases, you

can also find open-source software developed by communities of privacy activists. These tools are often sold anonymously to allow users to improve their security without worrying about being tracked.

Access to Uncensored Knowledge and Resources

- **Digital Libraries**: The Dark Web is home to several digital libraries that offer free access to books, research papers, and other academic resources. These libraries are often used by people who don't have access to traditional resources or by students who can't afford expensive textbooks. Many of these resources are not available on the surface web due to copyright restrictions or government censorship.
- **Sensitive Information Sharing**: Communities of researchers and activists use the dark web to share documents and information that would otherwise be censored or restricted. These documents may include government reports, research data, and documents exposing human rights violations. The dark web provides a secure space where this information can be stored and shared without the risk of being removed.

Opportunities for Cybersecurity Specialists

- **Vulnerability Testing and Penetration Testing**: The dark web provides a space for cybersecurity specialists to share information about vulnerabilities and attack techniques. This can be useful for security professionals looking to improve their skills in penetration testing and network defense. Of course, these activities must be conducted within the legal context and with the appropriate authorizations, but the dark web still offers a platform to learn more about and understand emerging threats.
- **Cybersecurity Training and Education**: Many experts share free educational resources and step-by-step guides on how to improve cybersecurity. These materials often include hands-on exercises, security tools, and tutorials that aren't readily available on the web surface. Cybersecurity specialists can benefit from these resources to deepen their knowledge and stay up to date on the latest threats and defense methodologies.

Risks of the Dark Web

Introduction to Dark Web Risks

The dark web is often associated with illicit activity, and for good reason: it's a place where not only privacy and anonymity are sought, but also where criminal activity proliferates. In this chapter, we'll look at the main risks you encounter when browsing the dark web. It is crucial to understand these risks to properly evaluate your actions and make informed decisions when exploring this part of the internet. Among the main dangers we find scams, malware, phishing attacks and even legal consequences. Having a detailed understanding of the risks is the first step in mitigating them.

Scams and Frauds on the Dark Web

- **Fraudulent Marketplaces**: Marketplaces on the dark web often contain listings for both legal and illegal goods and services, but it is extremely common to find fraudulent sellers. Many dark web users have reported scam experiences in marketplaces, such as payments made for products that are never delivered or counterfeit goods. Some scammers use fake reviews to appear trustworthy and attract more buyers, while others exploit the escrow system (a guaranteed mechanism in which payment is held by a third party until confirmation of receipt of the product) with the aim of scamming both buyers and sellers. Since the dark web operates anonymously, recovering money lost in these situations is almost impossible, and there are no authorities or regulations that can assist you. In addition, some marketplaces suddenly close without warning, taking away all funds deposited by users, a phenomenon known as 'exit scam'.
- **Illegitimate Services**: Another frequent risk is related to illegitimate services advertised on the dark web, such as hacking for hire, fake documents, credit card cloning, and DDoS attack services. Very often sellers take payment without providing any service or, in some cases, provide poor quality services that do not achieve the promised goals. The lack of regulation and the total absence of guarantees make these transactions highly risky. Even when the service is provided, users are still at risk of being reported to the authorities by the sellers themselves or tracked by competing buyers. In addition, the reputation built within the dark web is not enough to guarantee that a provider is trustworthy, as reviews can be manipulated and sites can be shut down at any time, making any form of complaint impossible.

Malware e Virus

- **Downloading Dangerous Files**: Many dark web sites offer downloads of pirated software, videos, music, documents, and other content that often contain malware. These files can infect the user's computer, compromising its security and making it possible for personal information to be stolen. Malware can include keyloggers, ransomware, spyware, or trojans designed to monitor user activity, record user credentials, or block access to data until a ransom is paid. In addition, some variants of malware on the dark web can have worm capabilities, meaning they can automatically spread to other devices on the same network, thus increasing the risk of an entire home or business infrastructure being compromised. It is crucial to avoid downloading files from unverified sources and always use up-to-date antivirus software to reduce the risks associated with these downloads.
- **Zero-Day Exploits**: Zero-day exploits can also be found on the dark web, vulnerabilities not yet known by software manufacturers. These exploits are sold and used to conduct large-scale attacks, making the dark web a threat to both individuals and organizations.

Phishing Attacks and Stolen Identities

- **Targeted phishing**: Phishing attacks are a common practice on the dark web. Users may receive deceptive links that appear to come from trusted sources, such as forum administrators or verified vendors, but which actually lead to fake pages designed to collect personal information, such as login credentials or financial data. These attacks often use social engineering techniques to make messages more believable, such as imitating language used in certain forums or using details that the user may recognize. This type of attack is particularly dangerous because it exploits users' trust in dark web platforms and can lead to a complete identity compromise. Once collected, personal information can be sold or used for further attacks, such as identity theft or blackmail. To protect yourself, it is essential not to click on suspicious links and always check the validity of sources before providing any sensitive data.
- **Sale of Stolen Identities**: The dark web is a focal point for the trade in stolen personal data. Information such as credit card numbers, login credentials, IDs, and even medical records are frequently put up for sale. This data is collected through phishing attacks, malware, or large-scale data breaches. Once sold, personal data can be used to commit identity theft, open bank accounts, obtain loans, or make purchases in the victim's name. The consequences for victims can be devastating, resulting in significant financial damage, lengthy battles to restore their identity, and potential legal problems. Health data, if compromised, can also lead to discrimination or extortion. It's crucial to understand that once data ends up on the dark web, it can be resold multiple times, exponentially increasing the risk of ongoing abuse and fraud.

Legal and Moral Consequences

- **Violation of Laws**: Many of the activities that take place on the dark web are illegal, and even just accessing certain sites can result in significant legal consequences. For example, viewing illegal content such as child pornography or terrorist propaganda materials, or purchasing prohibited substances such as drugs, weapons, or fake documents, can lead to investigations and interventions by law enforcement. These activities are monitored by specialized units of the cyber police and international agencies such as the FBI and Europol, which collaborate with each other to identify suspicious users and collect evidence even in anonymous networks. It's important to remember that dark web anonymity isn't absolute: misconfigurations, using insecure services, or simply linking activity on the dark web and the surface web can reveal your identity. Several police operations have led to the closure of illegal marketplaces and the arrest of users around the world, proving that even on the dark web, there are no complete guarantees of impunity.
- **Ethics of Using the Dark Web**: In addition to the legal implications, there are also moral issues related to the use of the dark web. While there are legitimate opportunities, such as defending freedom of expression, participating in or supporting illegal markets or other harmful activities can have serious consequences for society as a whole. Using the dark web therefore requires a strong awareness and a sense of responsibility.

Protecting Yourself from Dark Web Risks

- **VPN and Anonymity Tools**: Using a VPN in conjunction with Tor is crucial to add an extra layer of anonymity and protection. VPNs help mask the user's IP address, further reducing the chances of being tracked.

- **Don't share personal information**: Avoid giving out any kind of personal information while browsing the dark web. Sites may attempt to collect data for malicious purposes; So, keeping a low profile is essential.
- **Use Up-to-Date Security Software**: Make sure that your operating system and all security software are always up to date. This helps protect against vulnerabilities that could be exploited by malware on the dark web.
- **Disable JavaScript in the Tor Browser**: JavaScript can be used to launch attacks against the user and reveal their identity. Disabling it significantly reduces the risk of attacks that can be exploited through the browser.

Cybersecurity and Identity Protection

Introduction to Security on the Dark Web

Browsing the dark web comes with numerous risks, but with the right strategies and techniques, you can significantly reduce the danger and protect your identity. This chapter provides a practical guide to essential security techniques to minimize exposure to scams, malware, and other threats. We'll look at tools like VPNs, Tor, security software, and behavioral measures that can contribute to safe browsing. Identity protection is a crucial aspect, especially when using a network where trust is difficult to establish.

Malware Defense and Other Attacks

- **Antivirus and Anti-malware**: Using up-to-date antivirus and anti-malware software is crucial for reducing the risk of viruses, trojan, ransomware, and other forms of malware infection when browsing the dark web. Programs such as Bitdefender, Kaspersky, Malwarebytes or Norton are among the most effective at identifying and blocking known threats, protecting the device from possible exploits. Modern antiviruses not only scan the system in real-time for threats, but often also include advanced features such as behavior monitoring to detect suspicious activity, even from unknown malware. It's important to always keep your antivirus up to date to ensure that it can recognize the latest threats, as cybercriminals release new malware variants frequently. Additionally, it is recommended to schedule periodic in-depth scans and use web protection features to automatically block sites known to distribute malware.
- **Firewalls and Traffic Monitoring**: Using a firewall is another key measure to secure your connection. Firewalls act as a security barrier between your system and potential attacks from the outside, helping to filter incoming and outgoing traffic and blocking unauthorized access attempts. Software such as **pfSense** (an advanced open-source firewall) or even firewalls integrated into operating systems, such as the **Windows Defender Firewall**, can be configured to monitor connections in real time and alert the user of any suspicious activity. In addition, modern firewalls can be configured with advanced rules that filter traffic based on specific ports, IP addresses, or protocols, and offer **Intrusion Detection and Prevention System (IDPS)** capabilities, which can detect and block potentially malicious activity. These features are essential for protecting your system from more sophisticated attacks, such as those that exploit zero-day vulnerabilities or automated intrusion attempts. Properly configuring a firewall requires technical knowledge, but using step-by-step guides and supporting communities like pfSense can facilitate this process and make protecting your device much more effective.
- **Sandboxing**: To further reduce the risk of infection, we recommend that you use a virtual machine or sandbox environment to isolate browsing activity. This approach creates a barrier between the main system and the browser used to explore the dark web, preventing malware from infecting the entire system. An example of a sandbox environment is **Sandboxie**, which allows you to run the browser in a virtualized environment, isolated from the rest of the operating system. Alternatively, the use of **virtual machines (VMs)**, such as those created with **VirtualBox** or **VMware**, provides an extra layer of security, as the entire operating system is virtualized. In the event of an infection, the malware will remain confined to the VM, without being able to access the main system. For example, a user could set up a VM with a lightweight Linux distribution, use Tor to browse the dark web within this VM, and, once the session is over, simply delete the virtual machine, thus ensuring that any potential malware is destroyed. This approach is especially useful for

testing suspicious sites or applications, as the environment can be quickly restored to a previous state without risking compromise of the real system.

How to Recognize and Avoid Phishing and Scams

- **Recognize the Warning Signs**: Phishing attacks on the dark web often come in the form of urgent messages or incredible offers. Be especially careful with messages that require immediate action, such as clicking on a link or providing personal information. Always check the URLs of the sites you visit carefully and look for inconsistencies, such as spelling mistakes or strange extensions.
- **Identity Verification and Two-Factor Authentication (2FA):** Whenever possible, use two-factor authentication for your accounts. This measure adds an extra layer of security, as even if a password is compromised, a second factor will be required to access the account. Alternatively, some dark web platforms offer PGP verification keys for secure communications; It is always best to verify these keys and authenticate the sources.

Controlling Personal Information and Data Breach

- **Monitoring Your Data**: There are several services, such as Have I Been Pwned, that allow you to check if your personal information has been involved in a data breach. This type of monitoring is crucial to react promptly in case credentials fall into the wrong hands. On the dark web, stolen data can be sold and used quickly, so speed of action is crucial.
- **Encryption of Communications**: Using encryption tools such as PGP to protect your communications is essential to ensure that your data is not intercepted while you are browsing. End-to-end encryption, such as that provided by Signal for mobile communications, can be used to ensure that no third party can read messages.
- **Secure Password Management**: Passwords are often the weak point of online security. Using a password manager like Bitwarden or LastPass allows you to create and manage strong passwords without having to memorize them. It's crucial to avoid using the same password for multiple accounts, especially when dealing with accounts used on the dark web.

Improving Anonymity with VPN and Tor

- **Use of Reliable VPNs**: Using a VPN is imperative for ensuring anonymity while using the dark web. It's important to choose a reputable VPN provider that doesn't keep logs of user activity, such as NordVPN, ProtonVPN, or ExpressVPN. Connecting your VPN before launching Tor offers a double layer of protection, as it hides your use of Tor from your ISP (Internet Service Provider).
- **Configure Tor for Maximum Security**: Tor is a powerful tool, but it needs to be used correctly to ensure security. We recommend that you disable JavaScript in your enhanced security settings, as JavaScript can be exploited to perform fingerprinting attacks that could reveal information about your device, thereby compromising anonymity. Additionally, avoiding downloading files is essential, as these can contain malware and often require opening outside the Tor browser, which can reveal the real IP address. Using the highest level of security available in your Tor browser settings further reduces your risk by blocking potential vulnerabilities exploited by malicious sites. It's also not safe to use Tor to access surface web sites that require personal credentials, such as banking or social media, as this could compromise your anonymity, in part because these services collect user data that could be correlated to reveal your real identity. It's always best to use Tor only to access content that is compatible with anonymity and with an adequate level of security.

Using Secure Operating Systems

- **Tails and Whonix**: To ensure maximum security and anonymity, many dark web users use operating systems designed for privacy. **Tails** is a live operating system that can be booted from a USB stick or DVD and leaves no traces on the computer after shutdown. Tails uses the Tor network for all internet traffic, thus ensuring a high level of anonymity. In addition, Tails includes security tools such as KeePassXC for password management, OnionShare for secure file sharing, and the Thunderbird email client with support for PGP, which allows encrypted email communications. All the work done on Tails is only temporarily stored in RAM, and when you restart all activities are deleted, making it difficult to retrieve information. **Whonix**, on the other hand, is a Debian-based distribution that uses Tor for all internet traffic, providing a highly secure and anonymous environment. Whonix consists of two parts: the **Whonix Gateway**, which manages the connection to Tor, and the **Whonix Workstation**, which is used for all user activities. This dual-machine approach ensures that even if an application compromises the Workstation, the user's identity remains protected as all traffic is routed through the Gateway. Using these operating systems significantly reduces the risk of being tracked and ensures that all communications take place through secure channels, making Tails and Whonix ideal for those who need privacy protection at the highest level, such as journalists, activists, and users living in countries with heavy censorship.

Legitimate Opportunities on the Dark Web

Introduction to Legitimate Dark Web Opportunities

The dark web is often associated with crime and illegal activities, but there are many legitimate and positive opportunities within this hidden part of the internet. In this chapter, we will explore how the dark web can be used for legitimate purposes and how it can offer tools for freedom of expression, investigative journalism, and digital privacy. We will explore secure communication platforms, knowledge-sharing forums, educational resources, and channels for safe journalism.

Secure Communication and Source Protection

- **Whistleblower Reporting Platforms**: The dark web provides a safe space for whistleblowers – individuals who report misconduct or illegal behavior within organizations. Platforms such as **SecureDrop** allow you to send documents to journalists without compromising your identity, thanks to the use of the Tor network and end-to-end encryption. SecureDrop has been designed to minimize digital traces from both sources and journalists, thus ensuring a high level of anonymity and data protection. Major organizations such as **ProPublica, The Guardian,** and **The New York Times** have adopted SecureDrop to securely receive information from confidential sources. This form of communication provides greater security for those in risky situations, such as employees who want to report abuse, corruption, or rights violations, and allows sensitive information to be shared without fear of retaliation. In addition, the use of SecureDrop involves a rigorous authentication procedure using PGP keys, which ensures that only authorized journalists can access the materials sent by the sources.
- **TorChat and Other Communication Tools**: TorChat and other messaging tools available on the dark web allow anonymous communication between users. These tools use the Tor network to encrypt and anonymize messages, making it virtually impossible to track the sender or recipient. TorChat is a decentralized instant messaging application, which does not require central servers to operate, making it highly resilient against censorship attempts. In addition to TorChat, there are other alternatives such as **Ricochet** and **Cwtch**, which offer similar features, but with improved security architectures. **Ricochet** also uses the Tor network and allows communication without having to reveal any personal information, ensuring that users' identities remain anonymous. **Cwtch**, on the other hand, is an evolutionary tool that supports decentralized messaging and anonymous chatroom hosting, allowing users to communicate in groups without compromising their privacy. These tools are used by journalists, activists, and users in countries with severe restrictions on freedom of expression to communicate without being surveilled. In addition, these tools are designed to avoid the problem of communication metadata, making it difficult even to track information about when, where, and with whom the communication was made.

Knowledge Discussion and Sharing Forums

- **Technological and Privacy Forums**: The dark web hosts numerous forums where experts in cybersecurity, cryptography, and digital privacy share knowledge and discuss the latest technologies. These forums often provide information that is not available on the web surface, such as advanced privacy protection techniques or in-depth discussions of software vulnerabilities. For example, forums like **Dread** are popular for discussing topics related to privacy and security and can be a valuable resource for those looking to improve their technical skills.

- **Activist and Journalist Communities**: There are also communities where activists and journalists can meet virtually to discuss the issues they face and to exchange support. These communities help develop strategies to circumvent censorship, improve operational security, and promote awareness campaigns. In these spaces, freedom of expression is preserved and defended, allowing users to confront each other openly without fear of persecution.

Educational Resources and Digital Libraries

- **Online Libraries**: The dark web offers access to several digital libraries that contain a wide range of books, research articles, and educational resources that are often not available for free on the surface web. For example, platforms such as **The Imperial Library of Trantor**, **Library Genesis (LibGen)**, and **Sci-Hub** provide access to a vast collection of scientific publications, academic texts, and books on various topics. **Sci-Hub**, in particular, is known for offering free academic articles that are otherwise locked behind paywalls, thus allowing researchers and students from all over the world to access knowledge that would otherwise be limited. These digital libraries not only offer resources that would be economically inaccessible to many, but also allow knowledge to be preserved in contexts where access to information is subject to censorship or government restrictions. This can be particularly useful for students and researchers who do not have access to university resources, expensive scientific journals, or who live in countries with severe restrictions on access to information.
- **E-learning and Cybersecurity Courses**: Some dark web communities offer courses on advanced topics such as cybersecurity, cryptography, and penetration testing. While some of these courses may not have official certification, they are often created by industry experts and provide hands-on training in real-world techniques. These courses can be a valuable resource for those looking to enter the field of cybersecurity, learning from the professionals who actively work on these technologies.

Legal Markets and Earning Opportunities

- **Freelancing and Anonymous Consulting**: The dark web also offers the possibility of offering freelance services anonymously, such as IT security consultations or legal services for people who need assistance without wanting to reveal their identity. These services are often carried out through specialized marketplaces that facilitate the meeting between supply and demand in a discreet way.
- **Purchasing Digital Content**: In some dark web markets, you can purchase digital content, such as e-books and software, which may not be available on the surface web due to regional restrictions or censorship. Some of this content can be perfectly legal and buying it on the dark web guarantees greater privacy protection, avoiding the collection of personal data typical of conventional e-commerce services.

Using Tor for Safe Journalism

- **Access to censored sites**: For journalists working in countries where censorship is a serious problem, Tor offers access to information that would otherwise be blocked. The Tor network allows you to bypass blocks imposed by local ISPs and governments, allowing you to browse sites that are not normally accessible. In addition, many international news sites, such as **the BBC, Deutsche Welle**, and **The New York Times**, have .onion versions of their sites available on the dark web, allowing users to access news without restrictions and without fear of monitoring by authorities. These .onion sites are designed to offer the same experience as the surface web, but with a particular focus on user anonymity and privacy. In

this way, journalists and citizens can stay informed even in contexts where press freedom is severely restricted.
- **Posting Sensitive Content**: Tor and the dark web also offer the ability to post sensitive content that could be censored or lead to retaliation if posted on the surface web. Journalists can publish confidential documents or investigative reports without having to reveal their identity, using platforms like **OnionShare** to share documents securely.

Best Practices for Browsing the Dark Web Safely

Introduction to Security Best Practices

Browsing the dark web can come with numerous risks, but with the right security practices, you can minimize the dangers and protect your identity and data. This chapter will provide a step-by-step guide on security best practices for exploring the dark web, from using tools like Tor and VPNs to adopting prudent behaviors and advanced protection techniques. The goal is to ensure a safe and anonymous experience, without incurring the risks associated with illegal activities or surveillance.

Using Security Tools: Tor and VPN

- **Tor for Anonymity**: The Tor browser is one of the main tools for browsing the dark web. Using Tor allows you to encrypt your internet traffic and route it through a network of distributed nodes, making it difficult to track your online activity. However, to maximize Tor's effectiveness, it's essential to set your browser to safe mode, disabling JavaScript, and limiting the number of active plugins and extensions.
- **VPN for Enhanced Privacy**: Using a VPN in conjunction with Tor provides an extra layer of security. A VPN masks the user's IP address before traffic passes through Tor, making it even harder for an observer to tell that you're using Tor. It's important to choose a VPN that doesn't keep activity logs, such as **NordVPN, ProtonVPN,** or **ExpressVPN.** The combination of VPN and Tor (known as "Tor over VPN") helps protect your privacy against ISP monitoring and potential system vulnerabilities.

Security configurations for Tor

- **Disable JavaScript**: JavaScript poses a significant security risk on the dark web. Malicious scripts can be used to identify you or to carry out attacks that compromise anonymity. Disabling JavaScript in the Tor browser is a key practice to minimize this risk. You can do this by going to your browser's advanced security settings and setting the security level to "High".
- **Don't Download Files from the Dark Web**: Downloading files from the Dark Web is strongly discouraged. These files may contain hidden malware, which is designed to bypass Tor's defenses and reveal information about the user. If you need to download a file, do so inside a virtual machine (VM) or sandbox environment to isolate any threats.

Using Secure Operating Systems

- **Tails OS: Tails** is a live operating system that can be booted from a USB stick or DVD and leaves no traces on the computer after shutdown. Tails routes all internet traffic through Tor and includes security tools like **KeePassXC** for password management and **Thunderbird** for encrypted email. Using Tails is one of the best ways to ensure anonymity when browsing the dark web, as no activity is recorded, and all information is erased when the system is rebooted.
- **Whonix**: **Whonix** is another operating system designed for privacy that uses two virtual machines to ensure security. One virtual machine (the **Whonix Gateway**) routes all traffic through Tor, while the other (the **Whonix Workstation**) is used for user tasks. This isolation prevents compromises in the Workstation from revealing the user's identity, making Whonix a highly secure solution for anyone who needs anonymity.

Behavioral Practices for Safety

- **Don't Share Personal Information**: Sharing any type of personal information on the dark web poses a significant risk. It is essential that you never reveal your name, address, telephone number, or other identifying information. Using pseudonyms and maintaining an anonymous profile is essential to protect your identity.
- **Avoid direct financial transactions**: Financial transactions on the dark web can expose you to scams or compromise your anonymity. Use cryptocurrencies such as **Bitcoin** or **Monero** for transactions, but with caution. Monero is preferable for greater privacy, as it offers untraceable transactions and greater opacity than Bitcoin.

Advanced Security Tools

- **PGP for Encryption of Communications**: Pretty Good Privacy (PGP) is one of the most widely used tools for encrypting messages and files. In the context of the dark web, PGP is often used to ensure that email communications are secure and only readable by the intended recipient. It is important to generate a strong PGP key and keep it safe by using it to encrypt all sensitive communications.
- **Password Managers**: Use password managers like **Bitwarden** or **KeepassXC** to create and store strong, unique passwords for each service. This reduces the risk of brute force attacks and makes it difficult for bad actors to gain access to multiple accounts by compromising a single password.
- **Two-Factor Authentication (2FA):** Enabling two-factor authentication (2FA) on all services that allow it is an additional security measure. Even if a password were compromised, two-factor authentication would make it much more difficult for an attacker to access your accounts.

Metadata Control

- **Removing Metadata from Shared Files**: Metadata can reveal important information such as the author of a document, the GPS location of a photo, or the date the file was created. Before sharing any files on the dark web, it is advisable to remove this metadata using tools such as **MAT (Metadata Anonymisation Toolkit).** This is especially important for journalists and whistleblowers who want to share information without compromising their identity or that of their sources.

Real Stories from the Dark Web

Introduction to Real Stories

The dark web fascinates and scares at the same time, and it's often difficult to distinguish myths from reality. In this chapter, we will explore some true stories that testify to the various aspects of the dark web: from stories of scams and sensational arrests to stories of activists and journalists who have used the dark web for the common good. These real-life stories offer a clearer perspective on what the dark web stands for and the effects, both positive and negative, they can have on people's lives.

Silk Road: The Marketplace That Changed Everything

- **History of Silk Road**: **Silk Road** was one of the first and most well-known marketplaces on the dark web, founded by **Ross Ulbricht** in 2011. Silk Road revolutionized the way people could buy and sell drugs online, using Bitcoin for anonymous transactions. However, in 2013, Ross Ulbricht was arrested by the FBI and sentenced to life in prison without the possibility of parole. Silk Road was a symbol of the libertarian potential of the dark web, but also an example of the dangers of ignoring laws and participating in large-scale illicit operations.
- **Aftermath of the Arrest**: Ulbricht's arrest and the closure of Silk Road marked a turning point in the fight against crime on the dark web. Numerous other marketplaces, such as **AlphaBay** and **Hansa**, have attempted to fill the void left by Silk Road, but they too have been locked down in joint operations between several international security agencies. These events show that despite the anonymity promised by the dark web, the law can still reach those who operate on the dark side of the internet.

AlphaBay and International Collaboration

- **The Rise and Fall of AlphaBay**: **AlphaBay** was another major dark web marketplace that gained popularity after the closure of Silk Road. It offered not only drugs, but also fake documents, weapons, and malware. In 2017, AlphaBay founder **Alexandre Cazes** was arrested in Thailand in a joint operation between the FBI, DEA, and Thai authorities. Cazes was found dead in a Thai prison a few days after his arrest, in circumstances that are still not entirely clear today.
- **Cross-Country Collaboration**: The closure of AlphaBay was a pivotal moment in international cooperation against online crime. Authorities in several countries, including the FBI, Europol, and Thai law enforcement, worked together to track down Alexandre Cazes, using advanced cyber investigation techniques and cryptocurrency transaction monitoring. The investigation exploited methods such as blockchain tracking, which made it possible to follow the movements of Bitcoins used in illicit transactions. In addition, the authorities analyzed operational errors at Cazes, such as the use of personal email addresses in some of the initial communications related to the marketplace. This case showed how difficult it is for criminals to hide even on anonymous networks like Tor, especially when authorities collaborate globally and use coordinated investigation tools and innovative technologies to follow digital trails.

Stories of Activists and Whistleblowers

- **Edward Snowden**, the former NSA collaborator who exposed government mass surveillance programs, used tools such as Tor and other encryption software, such as **PGP**

(**Pretty Good Privacy**), to communicate securely with journalists and activists. Snowden also worked with trusted journalists, such as **Glenn Greenwald** and **Laura Poitras**, to ensure that his revelations were disseminated responsibly and safely. His revelations shook the world, leading to global awareness of the existence of large-scale surveillance programs by government agencies. His use of the dark web and anonymity technologies has shown how these networks can be crucial to defending freedom of information and privacy, especially in the context of increasing state surveillance. The anonymity technologies used by Snowden highlighted the importance of tools such as **SecureDrop**, which were later adopted by several organizations to protect communications with confidential sources.

- **Investigative Journalism with SecureDrop**: **SecureDrop** has been used by journalists to gather information from whistleblowers around the world. News outlets such as **The Washington Post** and **The New York Times** have used SecureDrop to obtain classified documents on corruption, financial crimes, and abuses of power. A case in point is the story of the **Panama Papers**, in which thousands of secret documents were shared via secure tools to reveal the extent of tax havens used by powerful people.

The Dark Side: Scams and Ransomware

- **Dark Web Marketplace Scams**: A classic example of a dark web scam involves selling substances that are never delivered. Many users have been scammed after paying in cryptocurrencies for non-existent goods, as there are no legal protections for these types of transactions. These scam sellers exploit the anonymity of the dark web to evade liability, making it impossible for victims to recover the money. One of the most famous scams was that of "**Exit Scams**", where marketplace managers suddenly closed the site taking away all the funds deposited by users. "Exit scams" have become a particularly common and lucrative phenomenon, especially during periods of increased commercial activity. These marketplaces raise funds for months or years, building a seemingly trustworthy reputation, only to then abruptly close and steal users' money. In addition to sellers, platform operators also use techniques such as fake reviews to build false trust among users, prompting victims to invest more before the final "exit".
- **Ransomware Attacks From The Dark Web**: Ransomware, such as **WannaCry** and **NotPetya**, has often been distributed via dark web networks. These attacks encrypt victims' data, demanding a ransom in cryptocurrencies to regain access. Ransomware can spread through phishing emails containing infected attachments or malicious links, and exploits vulnerabilities in operating systems to quickly propagate within corporate and home networks. Many of the ransomware distribution networks operate on the dark web, using marketplaces and forums to sell their software, user manuals, and even "Ransomware-as-a-Service (RaaS)" services that allow even the most inexperienced criminals to launch attacks. In addition, these forums offer technical support and guides on how to maximize the effectiveness of attacks, making ransomware a constantly evolving threat that is difficult for authorities to counter.

The Success of Online Security: The ProtonMail Case

- **ProtonMail and Privacy Protection**: **ProtonMail** is an encrypted email service that has often been used by dark web users to communicate securely. Founded by scientists at CERN and MIT, ProtonMail offers end-to-end encryption, ensuring that only the sender and receiver can read the content of emails, even the ProtonMail team cannot access the content of communications. ProtonMail uses advanced encryption techniques, and the entire service is hosted in Switzerland, which has some of the strictest privacy laws in the world. In addition, ProtonMail allows users to create accounts without providing any personal information, ensuring a high level of anonymity. It has become a critical tool for activists, journalists, and dark web users who need secure communication, especially in contexts where privacy is at risk or where government surveillance is a real concern. Despite the reputation of the dark web, services such as ProtonMail demonstrate how it is possible to provide legitimate and useful tools to improve global privacy, while also promoting freedom of information and the security of communications.

Prospects of the Dark Web

Introduction to the Future Prospects of the Dark Web

The dark web, a hidden part of the internet often shrouded in mystery and fear, will continue to evolve in the coming years. In this chapter, we will look at some of the prospects and changes expected for the dark web, both from a technological and social perspective. We will address topics such as the evolution of anonymity technologies, increasing government surveillance, legal implications, and how current trends could affect the future of the dark web.

Evolution of Anonymity Technologies

- **Increasingly Advanced Anonymity Networks**: The future of the dark web will largely depend on the evolution of anonymity technologies. Projects such as **I2P (Invisible Internet Project)** and the continuous improvement of the **Tor** network suggest that anonymity networks will become increasingly sophisticated. The goal is to increase the security and anonymity of users, making it more difficult for authorities and bad actors to track. The future could see the development of new networks based on decentralized technologies, such as **blockchain**, which would allow for greater censorship resistance and autonomous and distributed management.
- **Quantum Computing and the Challenge to Cryptography**: Another interesting perspective concerns the impact of **quantum computing** on the security of the dark web. Quantum computers could potentially break encryption methods currently in use, putting the privacy and security of communications on the dark web at risk. However, in parallel, researchers are developing **quantum cryptography** algorithms to counter this threat and ensure a new generation of security based on principles that not even quantum computers could easily breach.

Government Surveillance and Repression

- **Increased Surveillance and Advanced Investigation Techniques**: As the popularity of the dark web has grown, so has the interest of governments and security agencies in monitoring it. Authorities are developing **machine learning** and **artificial intelligence** techniques to analyze dark web traffic and identify suspicious activity. For example, cryptocurrency tracking tools are becoming increasingly advanced, and could make anonymity in transactions much more difficult. The future will see a growing tension between dark web users' desire to maintain privacy and government efforts to increase transparency and crack down on illegal activities.
- **International Cooperation**: International cooperation between law enforcement agencies is likely to increase further to fight crime on the dark web. Joint deals, such as those seen for the closure of **AlphaBay** and **Hansa**, will become increasingly common. Governments will work together to develop investigative tools that can circumvent anonymity technologies and to prosecute those responsible for illegal activities wherever they are in the world.

Evolution of Dark Web Marketplaces

- **Decentralized Marketplaces**: After the closure of many of the major dark web marketplaces, the trend may shift towards the adoption of decentralized models. The use of technologies such as blockchain and **DAOs (Decentralized Autonomous Organizations)** could allow the creation of marketplaces that do not have a single point of failure, making it much more difficult for authorities to close them. However, this would also increase the

level of risk and complexity for users, who would have to rely on smart contracts to ensure the security of transactions.
- **Increased Use of Privacy-Oriented Cryptocurrencies**: The use of cryptocurrencies such as **Monero, Zcash**, and other privacy-oriented currencies will continue to grow. These cryptocurrencies offer transactions that are much more difficult to trace than Bitcoin and are set to become the preferred payment method in dark web marketplaces. Monero has already become popular for its ability to hide senders, recipients, and transaction amounts, representing a major evolution in the fight to maintain anonymity.

Dark Web and Future Legitimate Opportunities

- **Freedom of Expression Platforms**: The Dark Web will continue to be an important resource for freedom of expression, especially in countries where governments censor the internet. Projects such as **SecureDrop** and other secure whistleblowing platforms will be able to evolve to offer even higher levels of security, allowing whistleblowers and journalists to communicate without fear of detection. It's also possible that new platforms will emerge, leveraging the latest technologies to ensure greater protection for sources and shared information.
- **Support Networks for Activists**: The dark web could become a hotspot for activists and non-governmental organizations looking for a safe way to coordinate their activities. By using technologies such as **mesh networks** to avoid traffic interception, the dark web could evolve into a robust platform to support communication between activist groups operating in hostile contexts.

Future Risks and Ethical Challenges

- **Increased Crime and Security Risks**: Unfortunately, as the dark web evolves, criminal activities are also likely to become more sophisticated. The increasing use of tools such as **Ransomware-as-a-Service (RaaS)** and the recruitment of professional hackers on anonymous forums pose a significant risk to global security. Cybersecurity authorities and companies will face new challenges to counter these threats and protect critical infrastructure.
- **Ethical Anonymity Issues**: The anonymity offered by the dark web will continue to be a complex ethical issue. While it provides a vital space for freedom of expression and protection against government surveillance, it can also be abused by criminals. The future will likely see an increasingly heated debate about how to balance the need for anonymity with the need to protect people from malicious activity.

Ethical and Legal Issues of the Dark Web

Introduction to Ethical and Legal Issues

The dark web represents a complex territory from an ethical and legal point of view, where the boundaries between what is right and what is wrong are often blurred. In this chapter, we will examine the ethical and legal challenges associated with the use of the dark web, exploring the moral dilemmas related to anonymity, freedom of expression, and the legal issues that arise in an attempt to regulate this hidden part of the internet. We will also discuss the legal tools currently employed to counter illegality and the implications of these efforts for user privacy.

Anonymity and the Ethical Dilemma

- **Anonymity as a Right or a Threat?** Anonymity is one of the founding principles of the dark web, but it represents a profound ethical dilemma. On the one hand, anonymity can be seen as a fundamental right that guarantees privacy and freedom of expression, especially in repressive contexts. It is an essential tool for activists, journalists and whistleblowers operating in authoritarian regimes, where free expression is punished. However, the same anonymity can be exploited for malicious activities, such as drug trafficking, arms sales, or the trade in stolen data. This creates a complex dynamic between the individual right to privacy and the need to ensure public safety.
- **The Impact on Victims**: The use of anonymity for criminal activities has a direct impact on the victims of these crimes. Scams, ransomware and illicit trafficking find a fertile environment on the dark web thanks to the cover of anonymity. Victims often find themselves without means of obtaining justice, as the perpetrators remain unidentified and out of reach of law enforcement. This makes the topic of anonymity even more controversial, raising the question of whether privacy protection is worth the price many people pay in terms of security.

Freedom of Expression and Legal Limits

- **Unrestricted Freedom of Expression**: One of the main attractions of the dark web is the ability to exercise freedom of expression without censorship. In many parts of the world, the internet is controlled and surveilled by governments, and the dark web provides an escape route for those who wish to express opinions without fear of retaliation. However, this total freedom brings with it risks, such as the proliferation of hate speech, terrorist propaganda, and violent content. Regulating freedom of expression on the dark web is an almost impossible challenge, and authorities often struggle to strike a balance between protecting individual freedoms and preventing abuse.
- **Abuse and Regulation Cases**: There have been numerous cases where freedom of expression on the dark web has been used to spread harmful content. Forums that promote terrorism, racism or hatred of certain social groups pose a threat to security and social cohesion. International regulations try to counter these phenomena, but the decentralized and anonymous nature of the dark web makes any intervention difficult. Defamation and hate speech laws are often unenforceable in this context, and even when content is identified, its removal becomes problematic.

Legal Issues and Government Actions

- **Legal Tools to Combat Illegality**: Law enforcement agencies use a combination of legal and technological tools to combat illegal activity on the dark web. **Infiltration operations**,

cryptocurrency tracking, and international collaborations are among the most common methods of trying to dismantle criminal networks. However, the effectiveness of these methods is limited by the difficulty of attributing online activities to real people and the use of advanced encryption techniques. Authorities are constantly trying to develop new strategies to address the challenges posed by the dark web, but any progress is often counterbalanced by the evolution of anonymity technologies.
- **Privacy Implications**: Government actions to monitor the dark web raise significant privacy issues. The surveillance techniques used to track the movements of funds and monitor network traffic can easily result in mass surveillance that goes beyond the confines of the dark web. This can lead to violations of the privacy of users who are not involved in illicit activities. Balancing public safety protection and privacy is a constant challenge for authorities and remains a major talking point in the context of dark web policies.

Case Studies of Legal Actions

- **Operation Onymous**: In 2014, law enforcement agencies in various countries launched **Operation Onymous**, a vast international operation aimed at shutting down numerous dark web marketplaces. This operation led to the closure of more than 400 websites and the arrest of dozens of individuals involved in illicit activities, such as drug sales and arms trafficking. The success of the operation was made possible by the cooperation between security agencies from different countries and the use of advanced investigative techniques to identify site managers. This case has shown that while the dark web is difficult to regulate, authorities still have the ability to successfully prosecute criminals, at least in part.
- **Silk Road case**: The closure of **Silk Road** and the conviction of **Ross Ulbricht** were emblematic examples of how the justice system can act forcefully against those responsible for the main dark web platforms. Ulbricht was sentenced to life imprisonment without the possibility of parole, a clear signal of the US government's intention to dissuade other potential operators from operating similar platforms. This case raised numerous ethical questions regarding the severity of punishment and the definition of justice in a digital context. Some argue that the sentence was overly harsh and represents an attempt to make an example of Ulbricht deter others, while others believe it was necessary to curb growing online crime.

Moral Issues and Responsibilities of Users

- **Individual Responsibility in the Use of the Dark Web**: An important ethical issue concerns the responsibility of users. While many people use the dark web for legitimate purposes, such as protecting privacy and communicating safely in repressive contexts, others choose to ignore the moral implications of their actions, participating in illegal markets or contributing to the proliferation of harmful content. Dark web users face accountability for their actions, and this raises the question of how aware they are of the potential harm their activities can cause to others. Anonymity does not eliminate moral consequences, and the ethical use of the dark web remains one of the biggest challenges facing the community.
- **Surveillance Ethics Debate**: As governments seek to increase scrutiny of the dark web to reduce illegal activities, there is intense debate over surveillance ethics. Many argue that surveillance is necessary to protect the public from the threats posed by organized crime and terrorism, but others believe that such measures constitute a violation of the fundamental rights to privacy and freedom. This debate is particularly relevant in an age when surveillance technologies are becoming increasingly invasive, and the risk of abuse by authorities is a growing fear.

Conclusions and Final Thoughts on the Dark Web

Introduction

The journey we have taken through the chapters of this book has led us to explore the dark web in depth, analyzing both its technical aspects and its ethical, legal and social aspects. We have seen how the dark web represents a complex reality, characterized by both positive and negative potential. In this final chapter we will reflect on what the dark web represents today, its possible future evolutions and the lessons we can learn from its use, not only in technological terms but also in ethical and social terms.

Duality of the Dark Web

The dark web is a clear manifestation of the duality of humanity and technology. On the one hand, it offers valuable tools to protect privacy and ensure freedom of expression in oppressive contexts. It is a place where activists can operate without fear of persecution, where journalists can communicate securely, and where ordinary citizens can explore information that would otherwise be censored. On the other hand, the dark web is a haven for criminals and illegal activities, who use anonymity to operate away from the laws and regulations of the surface web.

This duality is the feature that most represents the true nature of the dark web: a platform that is neither good nor bad, but which acquires value depending on the use you make of it. The same technologies that protect freedom fighters can be used by those who seek to violate the rights of others, and this raises profound questions about the nature of anonymity and privacy.

The Challenge of Regulating the Dark Web

Regulating the dark web is one of the toughest challenges of our time. On the one hand, governments want to limit the illegal activities that thrive in this environment, on the other hand, there is a need to protect individual privacy. Law enforcement operations, such as those that led to the closure of Silk Road and AlphaBay, show that the dark web is not entirely impenetrable, but they also highlight the limits of regulatory efforts. The ever-evolving anonymity technologies make it difficult for authorities to maintain control, and any attempt at regulation inevitably must contend with the possibility of restricting users' fundamental rights.

Technology and Ethics: A Delicate Balance

Technological progress is often faster than the ability to establish rules and ethical norms that govern it. The dark web is not an exception, but rather represents one of the most difficult fields to regulate due to its very nature. It is important for people to understand that every action has consequences, even if it is done anonymously. Anonymity technology must be used responsibly and consciously.

Educating users on the ethical use of the dark web is one of the goals that society should pursue. Whether they are activists fighting against censorship, or ordinary people seeking more privacy, everyone needs to be aware of the implications of their actions. Anonymity should not be an excuse to avoid responsibility, but a right that must be exercised in an ethical way and respectful of others.

Lessons for the Future

www.ingramcontent.com/pod-product-compliance
Lightning Source LLC
Chambersburg PA
CBHW031515210526
45464CB00007B/2919

The evolution of the dark web teaches us several important lessons. First, it reminds us of the importance of privacy in a world where surveillance is increasingly pervasive. The dark web is a warning against the excessive centralization of control over the internet, showing that there will always be a reaction when users' fundamental rights are put at risk.

Second, the dark web underscores the need for greater international cooperation to address the challenges of online crime. No country can tackle the problem of cybercrime hidden on the dark web alone. Collaboration between nations and the development of shared international regulations is essential to effectively address this global phenomenon.

Finally, the dark web invites us to reflect on the ethical consequences of technological progress. It is a call to responsibility, both for those who develop new technologies and for those who use them. The balance between innovation and regulation is fragile and requires continuous dialogue between legislators, technologists, and citizens.